To my wonderful angels,
my mom Mrs. Manly and my sister Mildred
who forever live in my heart.
To my sisters, brothers, family and friends
for your continued support.

Thank you for your phenomenal love and care!

- Sandra

A DIVISION OF S.E.M. INSPIRATIONALS, LLC

For information contact:
S.E.M Inspirationals Publishing House
1875 Century Park East, Suite 600, Los Angeles, CA 90067

ISBN Number: 978-0-9996139-0-0
Library of Congress Control Number: 2017917390

Author Contact Info:
Email: sempubhouse@gmail.com
FB: @SEMPubHouse
Company Page: @SEMpublishing
www.seminspirationals.com

Printed in the USA
Signature Book Printing, www.sbpbooks.com

RAISED UP BY
MRS. MANLY & HER
L'S

BY

SANDRA EVERS-MANLY
ILLUSTRATED BY WENDELL R. WIGGINS

As a child I, along with three brothers, two sisters, and ten foster children, was raised by our mother using some of her favorite words from one letter of the alphabet; that was the letter ....

Just like an at-home Sunday school lesson,
Mama taught us to love the one and the many:
love the Lord, love our family, love our community,
love who we are, and love what we do.
In spite of any situation,
we were taught to love anyway and anyhow.

Listen

We could not get by
without knowing how to listen.
Mother stressed that we had to listen
in many different ways and not just
with our ears. We had to listen with our eyes
in order to see the seen and the unseen.
Most of all, we had to listen with our hearts
in order to feel what was heard and unheard
in words spoken by others.

**In her daily lessons,
Mama would say we had to...**

Learn

Learn all you can while you can.
Know that learning takes place not just
in the classroom, but also in everyday life.
She taught us that some of the best learning
is what we learn from our elders,
our family members, and the paths we travel,
as we journey through life.

Sometimes when she had the idea that these lessons were not getting through she said, "You must **learn to listen and listen to learn.**"

Somewhere along the way –
Mrs. Manly – as she was affectionately known
by many – would add the words

Lift, Lean and Lead.

She told us to
lift others up and not tear them down.
She went on to say...
Lift others by doing our part
to make this world a better place, even if
it's just one corner or one chip of the world.

Lean

Coming from a Mississippi-born, civil rights family, my mom would say there would be times when we would find it necessary to lean on others, and there would certainly be times when others would have to lean on us.

Mama often reminded us of the importance to

It's not enough to sit on the sidelines,
she would say.
You have to help lead and bring about change.
She left us with the thought
that a good leader also knows
when and how to follow.
And, in the end, when to stand
and have a voice.

You got to Laugh

Laugh loudly and by all means keep smiling. Do not get so serious that you allow yourself to miss your blessings. Mama would say have some fun. Do not let anyone or anything steal your joy. Remember, there will be tough times. Tough times don't last, but tough people do. Laugh until your heart is content.

My mother never let a day go by without saying something about her L's. After all, it was the backbone of her in-home curriculum.

She would say, "You must be willing to live." Live life to the fullest today because tomorrow is not promised. Take time to smell the roses. Take care of yourself. She told us to live, let live and not take this life for granted.

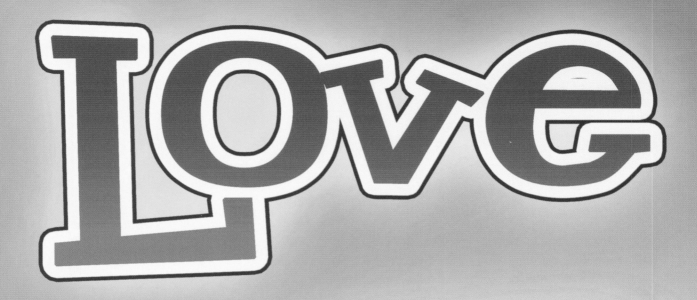

At the end of the day,
my mother often reminded me
and my siblings to continually reflect on the
greatest of the L's: love. When dropping me
off at my aunt's on her way to work, her
many days with me at the hospital during my
younger years, picking me up from school,
putting me to bed at night, sending me off
to college, and whenever we talked on the
telephone she would always say, "I love you.
I love you more than you will ever know."

When I became an adult,
my mother said that I had to
find my own letter to live and raise my family by.

I found that letter!

Thank you Mama, my angel and my blessing
I love you. I love you
more than you will ever know!

REFLECTIONS OF THE LETTER "L"

My mother did all she could to raise me well,
and **Live** my life by the letter "**L**."
So instead of worrying if I fail,
everything I do, I try to do it well.

Live with purpose,
Laugh with passion,
Look with focus,
Love everlasting.

Learn with an open mind,
Leap with a chance to shine,
Listen with my heart,
Link those who are apart.

Lead those in need of guidance,
Lift those in need of kindness,
Last longer when I'm in prayer,
I'm so thankful my mother cared.

I make mistakes, and sometimes I fall,
When I do I **Lean** on him who **L**oves us all.
Live your life laughing with those you **L**ove,
Lift your prayers to our **L**ord above.
Everything worth doing is worth doing well,
and if you do your best you'll never fail.

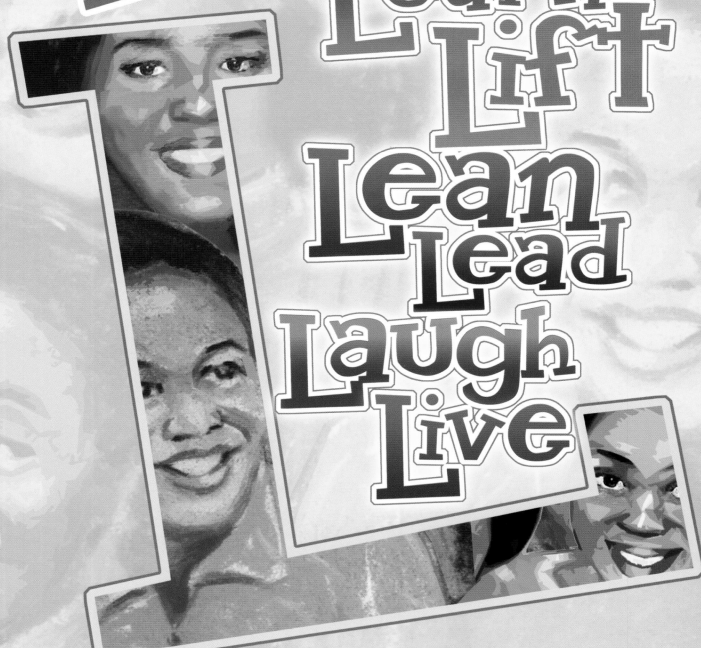

RAISED UP BY
MRS. MANLY
& HER
L's

Love
Listen
Learn
Lift
Lean
Lead
Laugh
Live

About Mrs. Manly

Born in Forest, Mississippi on March 6, 1925, Doris Evers-Manly was one of five children. Born a twin, she enjoyed the arts. Taught to sing by their father, the twins and their two oldest sisters were the first African American women to sing live on the radio in Forest in their group called the Evers Girls. Doris was known for her exceptional first soprano voice, her love for acting, writing, and was voted by her peers as the "girl who would never grow old." As a teenager during World War II, she often held rallies and sang to men deployed to war.

On a voyage for better opportunities, her journey led her to Pittsburg, California after attending Alcorn State University. In Pittsburg, she raised six children and was known for singing and whistling beautiful songs every morning while hanging clothes. Her melodic voice could be heard throughout the neighborhood, mesmerizing both young and old.

She worked 30 dedicated years at Pittsburg Senior High School. Upon retiring, the school named a section of the school and planted a rose garden in her honor. Mrs. Manly, as she was lovingly called, touched the lives of thousands of children throughout the world, many times allowing exchange students from India, Mexico, and Africa to spend time at the Evers- Manly home during the summer. Locally, she served as a recreation counselor, supervisor at the Boys and Girls Club, wedding planner and established the State Champion Sisters of Rhythm junior and senior girls drill teams. A passionate lover of *all* sports, she attended every sports event you can imagine.

If a child was in danger of abuse, the Pittsburg Police, Sheriff or Social Services departments brought them to Mrs. Manly's safe haven. She always had room for one more child and believed every child deserved to be loved. Because of her open heart and love for children, she opened her home to become an emergency foster mother, raising 10 foster children from diverse backgrounds.

Doris Evers-Manly raised her children by one letter – the letter "L." Not only did she teach her children about the letter "L," but she taught everyone she touched throughout her life of the importance of lifting others up and not tearing them down, being a leader, living life to the fullest, leaving a legacy and most importantly, finding time to laugh and always love.

RAISED UP BY MRS. MANLY & HER L's

About the Author:

Sandra J. Evers-Manly grew up in Pittsburg, California and currently resides in Washington, D.C. She is a sought-after speaker in the areas of diversity and inclusion, corporate responsibility, ethics and images in the media.

She has a strong commitment to working with young people to get them excited about education, especially science, technology, engineering, and mathematics; along with a comparable, enduring and demonstrative passion for keeping the arts alive in schools across the country.

Ms. Evers-Manly has received national recognition by numerous organizations for her commitment to the community, education, and working to increase diversity in Hollywood on screen and behind the scenes and helping to bring attention to the impact of gang violence.

She loves to tell people how she was raised by her mother's favorite words from the letter "L", and how they shaped how she lives today by words from her favorite letter "C": Character, Compassion, Conviction, Care, Commitment, Certain, Complete and Cherish to name a few. (everssa@yahoo.com)

About the Illustrator:

Wendell Wiggins grew up in Washington D.C. and was inspired by art at a young age. He received a BFA degree in Graphic Arts, Illustration and Photography from the Cleveland Institute of Art in Ohio. Wendell began his career as a storyboard and visual effects artist creating ideas for film and television projects. As a freelance artist he has provided services as a skilled muralist, computer animator, photographer, graphic designer and fine artist for a wide variety of major clients in the entertainment, corporate, film, music and publishing industries as well as having designed the logo for The African-American Film Marketplace and S. E. Manly's Short Film Showcase, the first of their many collaborations. (wigginsartdesign@gmail.com)